THE BARRIER REEF
AND NORTHEAST AUSTRALIA

A Land of Natural Wonders

Northeast Australia is a place of diverse and remarkable landscapes. A land of mountains and beaches, where tropical islands contrast with dense rainforests, savannahs and parched outback, and where nature is unsurpassed in the magnificent Great Barrier Reef, the jewel in Australia's wildlife crown.

T5-CUR-821

Contents

From rainforest to reef

Facts and figures

Each of Australia's six states has its own flag. Queensland, whose capital is Brisbane, has a British Blue ensign with a state badge – a Maltese Cross with an Imperial Crown at its center. Records state that the Maltese Cross was chosen as a symbol to represent the British colony rather than Queen Victoria's head, which would have been too difficult to reproduce on a flag.

Queensland is the second largest and third most populous state in Australia. Covering an area of over 668,207 square miles in the northeast of the country, Queensland is bordered by the Coral Sea and Pacific Ocean to the east and the Gulf of Carpentaria to the northwest. In terms of geography, climate, flora and fauna, this is one of the most diverse areas in Australia, and the world. Queensland boasts a total of five World Heritage sites, including the beautiful and extraordinary Great Barrier Reef.

Highs and lows

The dramatic landscape of Northeast Australia reflects the climatic differences of the region. Inland, the arid outback regions, such as Muttaburra and Longreach, lie in stark contrast to the savannahs and wet tropics of the central and northern areas. Bisected by the Tropic of Capricorn at the city of Rockhampton, the state is dominated by impressive mountains known as the Great Dividing Range, beginning in the state of Victoria in the south and ending in the tropical rainforests of Cape York Peninsula at the country's northern tip.

The 74 main Whitsunday Islands are surrounded by the Great Barrier Reef. The sparkling white sands of Hill Inlet surround some of the most spectacular scenery of all the offshore islands.

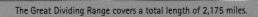
The Great Dividing Range covers a total length of 2,175 miles.

Country map of Australia (above), showing five of the six states (excluding Tasmania) plus the Northern Territory.

Did you know?

Once part of the great landmass Gondwanaland (right), Australia broke off nearly 150 million years ago along with India and Antarctica. Around 10 million years ago, the northern tip of Australia entered tropical waters, leading to a whole new range of life-forms, including reef-building corals.

Facts and figures

The Great Barrier Reef is the world's biggest coral reef and largest living structure. Comprising over 2,900 reefs and 940 islands and cays (small sand or coral islands), it covers 1,429 miles of coastline and a total area of 134,363 square miles.

A World Heritage Area and host to thousands of living species, the reef has no permanent human inhabitants; boats are moored here temporarily for marine research purposes only.

Queensland's outback consists of over 320,465 square miles of rugged terrain, characterized by red earth dotted with billabongs, which are stagnant lakes.

Area map (above) showing Northeast Australia's rugged coastline, including the area designated the Great Barrier Reef Marine Park.

Kangaroos outnumber Queensland's human population (of more than 4.2 million) by two to one!

Land of discovery

Did you know?

The 19th century was dominated by brutal clashes between British settlers and Aboriginal peoples as colonial land wars spread throughout Australia. The struggles in Queensland were some of the bloodiest, as Aboriginal people resisted British force, often attacking the homes of settlers (above). By 1900, many thousands of Aborigines and hundreds of colonists had died.

Archaeological sites suggest that Northeast Australia has been inhabited for at least 30,000 years. Early hunter-gatherers inhabiting the area included the indigenous Kuku Yalanji Aboriginal people of the Cairns region and the non-native Torres Strait Islanders, from the islands between Australia and Papua New Guinea, who were of Melanesian origin. The northeast region of Queensland was undiscovered by Europeans until the Dutch explorer Willem Janszoon landed on the shores of Cape York Peninsula in 1606, followed by his fellow countryman Jan Carstenszoon in 1623, earning Australia the name New Holland.

European discovery

Englishman Captain James Cook was the first European to discover the east coast of Queensland; in 1770, he made his famous voyage on the HMS *Endeavour*, exploring the Great Barrier Reef, where around 40 separate Aboriginal tribes were living. Cooktown, where he settled while repairs were made to his ship, now bears his name. Dutch, French, British and Portuguese settlers followed, as reflected in many of the region's place names.

Timeline

30000 BC	AD 1606	1623	1770
Archaeological evidence of Aboriginal people living in Northeast Australia.	Dutchman Willem Janszoon, sailing in the *Duyfken*, first charts part of Queensland's west coast, landing on February 26 by the Pennefather River in the Cape York Peninsula.	Dutchman Jan Carstenszoon explores western Cape York Peninsula around the Gulf of Carpentaria.	Captain James Cook in HMS *Endeavour* (right, a modern-day replica) annexes the east coast of Queensland on the grounds that it was *terra nullius* (no person's land).

In 1830, many Aboriginal peoples in Queensland were hit by smallpox, brought in by settlers.

HMS Endeavour, *the ship of the pioneering explorer Captain Cook (below), ran aground on the Great Barrier Reef on June 11, 1770. Supplies had to be thrown overboard in order to free the ship.*

Early inhabitants

One of the few indigenous tribes that continues to live as it has for thousands of years, the Kuku Yalariji people, also known as the Kuku Yalanji, were early inhabitants of the area now known as Port Douglas. Their distinct culture is uniquely adapted to their territory, which includes the Daintree Rainforest and surrounding river and coastal environments. They use rainforest plants and trees to make goods such as wooden shields, woven baskets and fish traps. It is estimated that they have lived here for 9,000 years, and the prehistoric rock art (above) in the town of Laura documents their cultural and historical links to the land.

1802	1859	1920	1982
First naming of reef by navigator, chart-maker and sailor Matthew Flinders, who names the southern area the Extensive Barrier Reef.	On June 6, Queen Victoria signs declaration establishing Queensland as a new colony, separate from New South Wales.	Qantas airline (*Queensland and Northern Territory Aerial Services Ltd.*) is founded, in order to serve Queensland's outback.	Eddie Mabo, a Torres Strait Islander and famous campaigner for Aboriginal land rights, starts legal action to claim rightful ownership of indigenous land in a landmark case, resulting in the Commonwealth Native Title Act of 1993.

Australia's pristine wilderness

The oldest forest

The Daintree Rainforest (World Heritage Site, 1988) is over 135 million years old, making it the world's oldest. At 463 square miles, it is also the largest area of tropical rainforest in Australia. Deep in the forest's heart is the Cooper Creek Wilderness, a privately owned World Heritage Nature Refuge. Densely packed trees are stabilized by the huge buttress roots (above) that are characteristic of the rainforest. The unique but fragile ecosystem of the Daintree Rainforest contains the highest number of rare and endangered plant and animal species anywhere in the world.

The landscape of Northeast Australia is extravagantly diverse. Sweeping great plains cover the dry and dusty outback, giving way to the pristine national parks and rugged peninsula of the north with its exotic rainforests, tropical islands and the rich coastal waters of the magnificent Great Barrier Reef. From Bundaberg, where the barrier reef begins, to tiny Bamaga on the tip of the Cape York Peninsula, the coast is dotted with a number of small towns, sugar plantations and cities, such as multicultural Cairns and the tropical city of Mackay.

Parks and forests

Queensland contains 470 protected areas, of which 216 are national parks; there are more protected parks than anywhere else in Australia. North of Cairns is the Daintree Rainforest, Australia's finest tropical rainforest (see box, left). The remote Lakefield National Park, on the Cape York Peninsula, is a beautiful wilderness of vast savannahs, stunning rivers and streams, and mangrove-covered coastal regions.

Whitehaven sand is so pure (99 percent silica) that it squeaks when walked upon.

Lakefield National Park

Queensland's second largest national park (after the Simpson Desert), Lakefield is 19,305 square miles of wilderness. Teeming with rivers and lagoons, the park is home to abundant birds and kangaroos, as well as freshwater and saltwater crocodiles. Dotted with eucalyptus and mangrove forests, the region is also known for its anthills (above), which can stand several yards high.

The sweeping coastline of Queensland, where rainforest and the ocean meet (left).

Kuranda

The picturesque mountain village of Kuranda is famed for its historic buildings and scenic railway, as well as the nearby attraction of Barron Falls (above), a spectacular gorge.

Mission Beach

Mission Beach (above) is a wildlife haven covering 8.7 miles of sandy coastline, bordered by the World Heritage sites of the Wet Tropics Rainforest and Great Barrier Reef.

Muttaburra

The outback town of Muttaburra (above) is located in 'fossil triangle,' one of the world's richest dinosaur repositories; *Muttaburrasaurus* dinosaur bones were first discovered here in 1963.

Wallaman Falls, in the Wet Tropics, has the longest drop of any Australian waterfall at 912 feet.

Phenomenal coral

The Great Barrier Reef lies at distances between 10 and 149 miles off the coast of Queensland in the Coral Sea, extending down about 1,430 miles from the Gulf of Papua to just below the Tropic of Capricorn. It is unique for its sheer size, scale and areas of special biological value. Although it is 500,000 years old, it has only existed in its present structure for 6,000 to 8,000 years, growing on top of the underlying structure of old reefs. When higher sea levels began flooding the coastal plain 20,000 years ago, the hills became islands where corals, linked by calcareous algae (containing calcium carbonate), flourished. This process eventually formed fringing reefs around the islands.

Perfect conditions

Over 400 species of coral are responsible for the reef's construction, their growth enabled by water currents with average temperatures ranging from 72–84°. The appearance of the Great Barrier Reef changes gradually, with long, thin ribbon reefs occurring at the northern parts on the continental shelf and broader platform reefs in the shallower southern waters, with their characteristic lagoons located at the center.

REEF TYPES AND FORMATION

Unlike atolls that form in deep ocean waters, most reefs of the Great Barrier have formed on the continental shelf. These include ribbon, fringing and platform reefs.

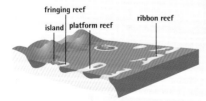

fringing reef
island | platform reef
ribbon reef

Ribbon reef

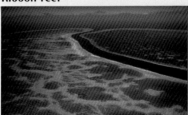

Ribbon reefs only occur in the northern part of the Great Barrier Reef, between Cooktown and eastern Torres Strait. This type of reef is so conducive to coral growth that the reefs can grow into high, narrow walls.

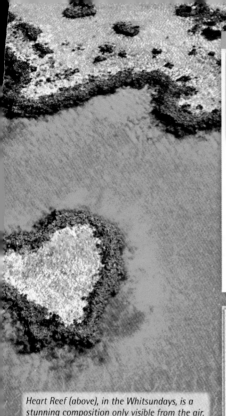

Heart Reef (above), in the Whitsundays, is a stunning composition only visible from the air.

Osprey Reef

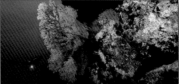

Not officially part of the Great Barrier Reef, the isolated Osprey Reef, with its unique topography and ecosystem, is an outstanding example of an oceanic reef. Its remote location away from fishing regions and human contact has saved it from the degradation that has affected reefs closer to shore, and its near-pristine condition means that it offers high scientific value as a marine research site for long-term monitoring.

Did you know?

North Queensland's pearling region has been farming cultured pearls (created by introducing a foreign body into an oyster shell) since the 19th century – they are renowned for their luster, size and quality.

Fringing reef

These reefs form in shallow waters close to the mainland. Much of the central reef is covered in plants, as opposed to corals, which are usually found toward the edges of the reef, where they can grow in abundance.

Platform reef

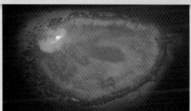

Platform reefs are found in the calm, shallow waters between the mainland and edge of the continental shelf. Flat and round, or oval shaped, they can be up to 6.2 miles long, and usually contain a lagoon.

A marine treasure

Did you know?

Amazingly, coral is both animal and plant. The animal part is a sea-anemone-like creature called a polyp. The plant part, a microscopic algae, lives inside the cells of the polyp.

A vividly beautiful underwater ecosystem that supports a vast array of species by providing them with food and shelter, the Great Barrier Reef is justifiably known as one of the seven wonders of the natural world.

Living wonderland

Host to a plethora of living things attracted by the nutrient-rich plants and waters, this unique wonderland is the world's largest World Heritage site (protected since 1981), bigger than the entire area of Italy. The reef's diversity reflects the maturity of its ecosystem, which has evolved over hundreds of thousands of years. It contains extensive seagrass and mangrove areas and one-third of the world's soft corals.

A home made of coral

The many caverns and crevices of the reef provide both shelter and home for a huge variety of marine life, from the red bass, which can live for over 50 years, to the rabbit fish, whose existence on the reef was unknown to scientists until 2008 when a number of sightings were made.

  Crown-of-thorns starfish pose a deadly threat to the reef: they eat coral faster than it can grow.

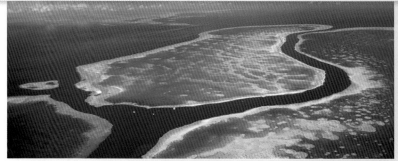

The tropical waters of the reef harbor an abundance of marine life, from beautiful, brightly colored fish and corals to turtles, whales and dolphins. Due to the abundance of species and the fact that new species are still being discovered, the figures given below are approximate.

Fish 1,500 species
Among the vast variety of fish found here is the lion fish (above). These beautiful but deadly creatures have elegant, elongated fins that also act as lethal spines.

Coral 400 species
Coral has been growing here for two million years. Hard reef-building corals form the external 'skeleton' of the reef in which the colorful soft corals bloom (above).

Mollusks 4,000 species
The giant clam (above) is the world's largest bivalve (a mollusk whose body is housed inside two hinged shells). Up to 3 feet 3 inches long, this creature can live for over 100 years!

Whales and dolphins
30 species
Whales appear in June and July, during the Australian winter. Dolphins (above) can be seen all year.

Birds 242 species
Eastern Reef herons (above) commonly nest on Heron Island. The reef also provides breeding grounds for ospreys, pelicans and sea eagles.

Sea turtle 6 species
The reef provides a valuable nesting ground for the vulnerable green sea turtle (above), one of only seven known tutles species.

Undersea worlds

Scuba diving

The spectacular coral formations, exotic marine life and amazing visibility of its warm waters makes the Great Barrier Reef unsurpassed as a location for scuba diving and snorkeling. Many operators within this thriving industry promote environmentally friendly excursions that minimize their impact on the ecosystem. It is estimated that this underwater world would take 10,000 years to fully explore.

Among the many weird and wonderful species that inhabit the waters of the Great Barrier Reef are the large (but generally harmless) whitetip reef sharks and the mysterious dwarf minke whales, which migrate to the reef every June and July, although it is not clear why, or where they come from. Some of the largest populations of the world's dugongs also live here; these huge creatures are more closely related to elephants than any marine mammals. The whole region is a diver's paradise with an unmatched variety of underwater species. Divers can often encounter the solitary potato bass, an ornately colored butterfly fish, or a tiny seahorse anchored to coral.

Into the deep

Further down on the seabed live the orange and white clownfish that share a symbiotic relationship with the anemones, which they clean and protect by eating algae and chasing away predators. Prawns, sponges and sea cucumbers also live among the seagrass and soft corals.

Dwarf minke whale

The dwarf minke whale is found only in the Southern Hemisphere. Like a dolphin, it can jump high from the water. It is found near the northern Great Barrier Reef in June and July.

Whitetip reef shark

Identified by a white tip on the top of its dorsal fin, the whitetip reef shark is timid and harmless to humans. It feeds on octopus, spiny lobsters and bony fish.

The gentle dugong (below) is an endangered species but is still legally hunted by Aboriginal people, for whom it is a traditional foodstuff.

Did you know?

Common at the northern reefs is the cuttlefish – in the class of mollusks called cephalopods, which are the most intelligent invertebrates. These creatures have three hearts, green blood, and can change their skin color and texture. They have eight arms and two tentacles with which to snatch prey.

A land of plenty

Brushtail possum

Common wombat

Short-beaked echidna

Australia's geographical isolation gives it a diverse and unique wildlife population. Northeast Queensland is home to hundreds of bird, reptile and frog species, and over 200 mammal species, mostly marsupials. These include two tree-kangaroo species that live exclusively in the Wet Tropics rainforests: the rare green possum and the iconic koala – a tree-dwelling herbivore often mistakenly called a bear. Many bat species are found here exclusively, such as the spectacled flying fox, so-called for the distinctive fur markings around its eyes. Northeast Australia is also home to the only two monotremes (egg-laying mammals) in the world, the platypus and the echidna.

Scary monsters

While the region has its share of dangerous creatures, such as freshwater and saltwater crocodiles and many snakes, introduced species have caused the most harm. Cattle have been successfully integrated for generations, but rabbits, feral cats and pigs, and especially toxic cane toads – introduced to control the destructive cane beetle – have caused immense damage to Australia's native flora and fauna.

Marsupials – Australia's dominant species

Instead of carrying developing infants in the uterus and feeding them via the placenta, like placental mammals, marsupials carry their infants in a pouch after birth following a short gestation period. Evolution has led marsupials to become the dominant mammal species in Australia. One hundred and forty species are found here and nowhere else on Earth, including kangaroos, wallabies, bandicoots, possums and wombats. Queensland's Wet Tropics are also home to the native tiger cat, or quoll, a fierce predator with a spotted tail and Australia's largest marsupial carnivore.

Koala and human fingerprints are so similar that a microscope can barely distinguish between them!

The red kangaroo (left) is the world's largest marsupial, but its babies (joeys) are born the size of a cherry, with the males maturing at two years of age. Adults gather in 'mobs,' and can travel at speeds of up to 35 miles per hour.

Feathered friends

Around 600 bird species are native to the region, including the rare golden bowerbird. Sadly, many – such as the cassowary – are endangered.

Kookaburra

The blue-winged kookaburra (above) is found throughout the region in tropical forests and eucalyptus woodlands. Known for its trademark cackling 'laugh,' it feeds primarily on snakes and large insects, but has been known to eat the odd small bird.

Cassowary

This spectacular, large flightless bird with a dangerous kick is native to the Wet Tropics. Like the kiwi and emu, it belongs to the Ratite family and has existed for 100 million years, but now fewer than a thousand exist.

Red kangaroos can cover a distance of 26 feet in a single leap.

Fragile beauty

Research ships

Important conservation and scientific research projects around the reefs are undertaken by specialist ships that also offer scuba diving expeditions and outings to the public. One such vessel is the *Undersea Explorer*, whose ongoing work includes the tagging and research of the rarely seen nautilus (above), a mollusk that once ruled the oceans as a giant predator.

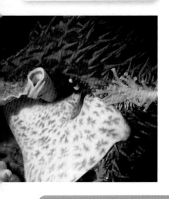

The Great Barrier Reef is an outstanding example of biological diversity in a setting of unparalleled beauty, but it is also a fragile ecosystem. Global warming (particularly the effects of El Niño) – and the resulting rise in water temperature – is considered the main environmental threat to the reef, because of the devastating consequences of coral bleaching, which can ultimately cause the death of a reef (see coral facts box, right). Crown-of-thorns starfish are voracious coral predators; by preying on coral polyps, each starfish is able to consume up to 64.5 square feet of living reef per year, making an outbreak potentially disastrous.

Oil and water

Pollution from shipping waste and oil leaks also poses a significant threat, and despite oil drilling not being permitted, 282 oil spills occurred in the area between 1987 and 2002. Even with protective measures in place, illegal fishing is still a problem, not only polluting the waters of the reef but also affecting the food chain. The giant triton (sea snail), the natural predator of crown-of-thorns starfish, has been overfished, making an outbreak of these destructive starfish more likely. On a positive note, many areas of the Great Barrier Reef are still in very good condition, but constant protection is required to ensure its stability.

A giant triton consuming a crown-of-thorns starfish (left). This sea snail can grow to almost two feet in length, making it an easy catch for local fishermen.

There are more than 30 historic shipwrecks in the Great Barrier Reef area.

Government concern

The national and state government are working together to ensure conservation of the reef. Ninety-eight percent of the World Heritage site is within the Great Barrier Reef Marine Park, a protected zone since 1975. The park's Species Conservation Unit works alongside Aboriginal communities and Torres Strait islanders to conserve both the natural and cultural heritage of the region.

Environmental awareness

Commonwealth legislation stipulates a number of specific measures to conserve and manage the marine park, including prohibiting mining and regulating fishing. Environmental issues are also covered by Australia's Environment Protection and Biodiversity Conservation Act of 1999.

Global warming can increase water temperatures; an increase of only 1.8–3.6° for six weeks can trigger coral bleaching – any longer and corals will die.

Healthy hard coral (above) retains its color. But if stressful environmental conditions strike a coral colony, the polyps expel the algae that provides color and essential nutrients, making the coral pale (bleaching). In 2006, coral disease struck the healthiest sections of the reef; seven disease types have been recorded here, caused by differing factors such as parasites, fungus and bacteria. Researchers have now conclusively linked disease severity and sea temperatures.

A researcher photographs and records damaged coral (below) off the Keppel Islands after a severe bleaching outbreak.

A land of adventure

In 2007, 2.2 million international visitors were welcomed to Northeast Australia and more than $7 billion was contributed to Queensland's registers. Aside from the obvious appeal of the Great Barrier Reef, Northeast Australia offers attractions as diverse as its landscape for the tourist. Holidays are more than just sun, sea and sand.

Culture and adventure

Guided tours through the rainforests and Wet Tropics are a speciality, and adventures abound, from bungee jumping to small-plane trips across the outback. The lure of the Great Barrier Reef makes tourism the principal commercial industry here, with marine activities ranging from scuba diving and snorkeling to fishing and glass-bottomed boat excursions. Culturally, the region offers everything from Aboriginal heritage sites and prehistoric artifacts to thriving cities such as Cairns or Mackay, close to the dazzling beauty of the Whitsundays.

The Tropical North

Queensland is dotted with charming coastal towns and cities such as Cairns (right), known as the gateway to the Great Barrier Reef. Mackay on the Whitsunday coast is one of the region's hidden gems; along with a botanical garden and fine marina, its historic center also boasts an outstanding collection of well-preserved Art Deco buildings.

The hottest temperature ever recorded in Australia was 127.4° at Cloncurry, Queensland, in 1889.

Cape York Peninsula has a rich Aboriginal heritage, with prehistoric rock art caves and sacred sites such as Mossman Gorge, traditionally owned by the Kuku Yalariji people. The Laura Aboriginal Dance and Cultural Festival, where indigenous dancers in body paint perform (below), is one of the most spectacular celebrations of Aboriginal art and culture.

Cattle farming in the outback has expanded into the tourism sector. For an authentic experience, many ranches now offer tourists the chance to enjoy a 'farmstay' - albeit in luxury - in an authentic cattle station like the one pictured here.

Barrier reef challenge

How much have you learned?

1 Why is Osprey Reef especially useful for scientific monitoring?

a: It houses the largest population of clown fish in Australia
b: It is the largest of all the reefs
c: Its remoteness has spared it from degradation

2 Why were Aboriginal women originally used as pearl divers?

a: The women have better vision underwater
b: The women have a bigger lung capacity
c: The men were away hunting on land and often absent for long periods of time

4 Why was 'fossil triangle' so named?

a: Because a fossilized ancient fig tree has been found in the region
b: Because a large repository of dinosaur bones has been discovered in the area
c: Because three ancient aboriginal settlements have recently been uncovered there

5 What is unique about the Daintree Rainforest?

a: It is the biggest rainforest in the world
b: It is the oldest rainforest in the world
c: It is the wettest rainforest in the world

Picture This

3 Which fish helps clean and protect the sea anemones in the Great Barrier Reef?

a: The clownfish
b: The potato grouper
c: The seahorse

19th-century Queenslanders traded dried smoked sea slugs with the Chinese in exchange for tea.

6 Who was the first Englishman to discover Queensland?

a: Captain Arthur Phillip
b: Matthew Flinders
c: Captain James Cook

7 What is the size of a newborn red kangaroo?

a: About the same size as a coconut
b: About the same size as a cherry
c: About the same size as a watermelon

8 Why does the cuttlefish change color?

a: It changes when it is too hot or too cold
b: It changes depending upon its mood
c: It changes when it feeds

9 From where does the dugong gets its name?

a: The Malay word for donkey
b: The Malay word for mermaid
c: The Malay word for elephant

10 The huge roots of this Daintree Rainforest tree are known as:

a: Buttress roots
b: Cable roots
c: Fortress roots

11 Mackay is known for its outstanding examples of which architectural style?

a: Art Deco
b: Art Nouveau
c: Neo-Gothic

12 Which Queensland resident bird is endangered?

a: The kookaburra
b: The sacred kingfisher
c: The cassowary

14 What is distinctive about monotremes?

a: They are egg-laying mammals
b: They are flying marsupials
c: They are swimming reptiles

15 Which disease decimated the native Aboriginal population?

a: Cowpox
b: Chickenpox
c: Smallpox

Picture This

13 Which is mainland Australia's largest marsupial carnivore?

a: The quoll
b: The koala
c: The red kangaroo

Captain Cook named Cape Tribulation, where his ship ran aground, 'because here began all my troubles.'

16 What was unique about Queensland's 19th-century education system?

a: It held classes seven days a week
b: It was the first to employ non-clerical teachers
c: It was free

17 Which coastal city in Queensland is known as the gateway to the Great Barrier Reef?

a: Cairns
b: Mackay
c: Sydney

18 What kind of creature is the spectacled flying fox?

a: A bat
b: A glider
c: A squirrel

19 Which beach has sand that is 99 percent pure silica?

a: Whitehaven Beach
b: Mission Beach
c: Bondi Beach

20 How old is the present structure of the Great Barrier Reef?

a: 6,000 to 8,000 years
b: 18,000 to 20,000 years
c: 490,000 to 500,000 years

Answers

1: (c). Despite its remote location, the Osprey Reef's pristine conditions make it a popular destination for divers.

2: (b). The only way to distinguish a natural pearl from a cultured pearl is by use of X-ray.

3: (a). Along with certain damselfish, the clownfish is the only species of fish that can avoid the poison of a sea anemone.

4: (b). Australia's largest dinosaur fossil, standing 13 feet high and 53-69 feet in length, was discovered in the triangle in 2001.

5: (b). Covering only 0.2% of Australia's landmass, Daintree Rainforest is home to 30% of the country's frog, marsupial and reptile species.

6: (c). Captain Cook ran aground on the Great Barrier Reef – delaying his voyage by seven weeks.

7: (b). Female red kangaroos have a blue-tinted coat, earning them the nickname 'blue fliers'.

8: (b). Cuttlefish have ink, like squid and octopuses. This ink was formerly an important dye, called sepia.

9: (b). Dugongs are sometimes known to breathe by 'standing' on their tail with their heads above water.

10: (a). The Daintree Rainforest was named after the Australian geologist and photographer Richard Daintree, who was the first to discover gold in Queensland.

11: (a). An international design movement spanning the 1920s to the late 1930s. Famous examples of Art Deco buildings include New York City's Empire State and Chrysler buildings.

12: (c). The fruit-eating cassowary has been named the most dangerous bird in the world in the Guinness Book of Records, because of its strong leg kicks which can prove fatal to humans.

13: (a). Native to Australia and parts of Papua New Guinea, the quoll or tiger cat belongs to the genus 'Dasyurus', meaning 'hairy-tail' in Latin, which also includes the Tasmanian Devil.

14: (a). The egg is retained for some time within the mother, who provides it with nutrients.

15: (c). Up to 50% of the Aboriginal population was wiped out by smallpox.

16: (c). The first-ever school in Queensland opened in 1826, two years after the first settlement was established.

17: (a). Tourists can also find heritage sites and prehistoric artifacts nearby as well as the Daintree Rain Forest.

18: (a). Also known as the spectacled fruit bat, this species is also found on New Guinea and neighbouring islands. Predators include crocodiles and the white-breasted sea eagle.

19: (a). Whitehaven Beach is on Whitsunday Island, the largest of all the islands in the Whitsundays.

20: (a). More than one third of the coral on the reef reproduces sexually during an annual mass spawning event. This always occurs during the night.

Useful websites

http://www.wwf.org.au/ourwork/oceans/gbr/ The conservation work of the WWF in the Great Barrier Reef Marine Park.

http://www.rrrc.org.au/ Scientific research on the Great Barrier Reef and North Queensland rainforests.

http://www.daintreerainforest.com Fascinating site about the Daintree Rainforest.

Staghorn coral has more species and is the fastest growing of all corals on the Great Barrier Reef.